The Way of the Wind

Poems by Ken Hada

First Edition: March 2008
Published by Village Books Press
Cheyenne: OK 2008
ISBN:13: 978-0-9791510-7-1
10: 0-979-1510-7-4

Copyright Ken Hada, 2019: All Rights Reserved. No portion of this book may be reproduced in any manner whatsoever without written permission from the publisher, except for brief excerpts for review purposes.

Printed in the United States of America

SECOND EDITION
Fine Dog Press
Morris, Oklahoma
ISBN: 978-1-7339795-4-2

Contents

IN THIS RESOLUTE PLACE

The Witness Tree / 11
We Have These Witnesses / 12
The Old Home Place / 14
The Windmill / 15
Building Barbed Wire / 16
Wind and Rain / 17
Cedar Grove / 18
The Promised Land / 19
Prairie Song / 20
The Smell of Rain / 21
Dressing Catfish / 22
Fishing Dock / 23
Red Tail Hawks / 25
Indian Paintbrush / 26
Rock Creek / 27
Worship / 28
The Tornado / 29
Cousins at Play / 30
Forbidden / 31
Little Boy Shucking Corn / 32

WILD RED DARKNESS

Echoes / 39
Blue River / 41
What We Have Lost / 42
Summer Moon / 44
Summer Squall / 45
The Fire Girl / 46
Shadows Across Junipers / 47

Pastels / 48
Creek / 49
Of Streams / 50
Thus the Dust / 51
Gone by Morning / 52
Late Summer Nights / 53
Sleeping Out Under Stars / 54
Nearly Angels / 55
Forest Song / 56
November Night / 57
BlackJacks Late in Winter / 58
Cimarron / 59

SINGING OF TRANSIENCE

Birth Song / 67
The Wounds of Oklahoma / 68
In Memoriam / 69
Horses Grazing in a Country Cemetery / 72
Funeral Song / 73
Requiem for the Wounded / 74
Moonlight / 75
Red Dirge / 76
Tree Frogs / 77
That Which Clings / 78
Of Desire: or What Foxes Do / 79
River Song / 81
Grace Strokes / 82
What Wind Takes / 83
Winter Stories / 84
Compensation / 85
Wind Song / 86

for Duane,
    for Debbie

In This Resolute Place

You don't know which way the wind blows
so how can you plan tomorrow?

— Annie Herring

The Witness Tree

In a meadow of buffalo grass
and cedar groves, a bur oak survives
more than three hundred years
in timeless red earth. This solitary
old man has lived through storms,
broken dreams, promises gone unfulfilled.
Drovers and Natives rendezvoused
here to exchange gifts for grazing rights.
Lovers have picnicked under his canopy.
More than one drifter has sought wise
counsel under the impressive limbs.
This grand survivor has much to say:
witness to the Land Run, to statehood,
witness to our sins and to our hopes.

We Have These Witnesses

These men
these gnarly men
with twisted frames
sun-slant eyes
grizzled hair

These men
squatting heel to heel
in a wheat field at sundown
remembering tomorrow's burden

These men
witness to my future
witness to a land
that vows to break them
to wind that won't let them be

These women
who bore hope
with quilting hands
hammered forearms
that look good still
in a Sunday-red dress
with a pink rose

These women
who notice the flycatcher in flight
who snap garden beans
and wring necks of fryers
plow October ground
in alternating furrows
of hope and doom –
hope and the alternative
too dark to consider
too bleak to imagine

These witnesses
Immigrants
stalking freedom like predators
building community
like fire ants in usurped soil
living beyond the fenced lines
of failure and success
determined by work
wedded to a new land
haunted by the "Old Country"

Return like sunflowers
gritty and God-fearing

The Old Home Place

Still it stands: with a rumpled roof
of eternal tin, reminding me
of Hungarian pilgrims who sought
a home like seeds need soil

who farmed stubborn red land
with her enchanted past of tribes
before the plow, buffalo wallows
signify secrets in the grass

along a creek where Time whispers
in gypsum beneath purple thistle
that feeds flycatchers and quail
alongside these adobe walls.

A family sheltered through bitter
cold nights, hands parched blue
from plowing in prairie wind, pain
begetting pain in Autumn rain.

Knowing little of the land's soul,
wheat teased them – saying they might
make it after all – after locusts, drought
and hail humbled, hardened

and left them at the severe mercy
of a sun settling on broken
creosote poles that once framed hope
in this resolute place.

The Windmill

creaks and groans
the belt squeaking in prairie wind
wrinkled blades twirling
in tired momentum
unbalanced.

Thirsty calves moan
as I rinse in prodigious water
trickling faithfully
from a black pipe at the end
of a pulley drawing water
from a sparse, specious land

an angel hovering in empty sky
still turning water into life.

Building Barbed Wire

He taps the last staples in a corner post
grounded in good known earth

after stretching wire tight enough
for wind to play its tune –

bent and bowed at sundown –
an existential thing for any cowboy.

He raises a plastic jug, splashes leftover water to
satisfy his grateful upturned face

before pissing in open pasture – his field,
his place – nothing really feels better.

Glancing over a stooped, sun-burned shoulder,
he reassures a tenuous homeward walk.

Wind and Rain

Everything's harder in the wind
Cal said
and he would know

Plowing's harder
Pissing is harder

Hell, even praying is harder in the wind
Cal said

and he would know

His boy came into the world one blustery
October morning when he stepped outside to piss

He congratulated the wife then went back to plowing
mooring hard against time
pulling hope against the wind
trying to keep his furrows straight

the wind blew all week, then howled into rain
the rain assaulted his field another week
filling his furrows full of despair

now his plow stands still stuck
in violent red mud that smacks his boot-top

he falls to his knees calling the Lord God-a-Mighty
to let him get his seed into good soil
to not let his seed go to rot

Cedar Grove

Western cedars
along tall
grass-filled prairies
frame my life.

Surviving change,
a seedy
overgrown place
harbors me.

Musing in wild
transcendence,
buoyant bluebirds
sing me back.

The Promised Land

Wind slices me
like a buck knife,
dwarfed cedars veiling me.

Embracing a steel rifle barrel
I wait, huddled in place
hunting deer, matching wits
with a superior beast,
balancing conflicted instincts
in this harsh land
my ancestors settled.

They came in wagons,
some came on foot
carrying only a future.

Burrowed beneath wind
two ladies grew old together
surviving in a sod dugout,
determined like rodents
below a carving wind
in this auspicious land.

Prairie Song

Endless miles open
before me,
invite me to follow wind
swaying through buffalo grass
down a gully
where cottonwoods and cedars
hold a creek-bed.

I follow as I am led
by wind and sun
arced above,
gypsum and sandstone
below – purple thistle,
ragweed, wild plum
and prickly pear.

The miles seduce me:
each step brings me closer,
rewards me
like scissortails
in ecstasy of flight.

The Smell of Rain

I smell rain stirring
in humid air,
dusty pollen
carried on wind,
life and death mingled.

I smell rain taking me back
to childhood,
standing on a hill
overlooking a valley
I would sniff moist air
and ride breezes
across the expanse
over a creek-bottom.

Hawks and vultures soaring
on updrafts
envied me,
envied my freedom,
my escape,
even as they would rise
and fall
and rise again
hundreds of feet at a time
without flapping a single wing.

Dressing Catfish

Grandma used to dress catfish,
that's how she said it.
Her large calloused hands gripped
pliers and the head
and pulled hard in opposite directions
until the skin grudgingly yielded
to her strength.

Then she grabbed her butcher knife,
the one she used to dress chickens,
that's how she said it,
and slit the belly
and circumspectly fingered out entrails
under a running spigot
before she finally chopped off the head.

Those virile death-hands held
firm the soft slippery victims,
those same hands that felt
my fevered forehead,
and touched my sunburned shoulders.

Fishing Dock

These planks extending
like a tee into water
hold me above water,
water which I cannot know
below me except
what I bring to surface
with rod and line
except that which shows
itself for a moment
like a splashing carp
or sand bass.

But here above water
there are whispers
where wind laps water
against barrels
supporting this frame.

Whispers across the water.

Secrets I share sitting
beneath a half moon
looking hard at sagging line
in dim glow of lantern light –
the smell of bait,
a grunting heron,
somewhere out there
an owl hoots.

I touch my hands
where hooks have stabbed me,
where catfish have finned me,
the bloody stinging
will last a good many days
but I don't mind wounds
from this place –
part of the ceremony
in this private sanctuary
I enter, and in deep night,
realize with somber contentment
that few things in life
come without pain.

Red Tail Hawks

Perched on higher limbs,
proudly superior,

they scan horizons
missing nothing,

white chests protruding,
talons sharp, beak poised

to launch earthward
for the swift patient kill.

Indian Paintbrush

We can agree concerning
their beauty:
crimson
like pure sin.

Master designer,
random process?
Neither satisfy
the demands of intuition.

But we can agree
about beauty
and we can agree
that beauty

trumps ignorance
and ignorance
is all we know
with certainty.

Rock Creek
(Tulli Abokoshi

Rocks speaking
across quiet water
welcome me
back to this place
I must have visited
lifetimes ago.

I meet myself, again,
Reflected —
and know the truth
of being found out,
the humility
of being known.

Worship

Stars shine past Time.

Vision and knowing
share common space,
my awareness limited
only by vapidity.

Above me
stars swim endlessly.

About me
horizons glisten in the darkness.

I sit on a sandbar
feeling creek-water trickle.

Time and Being
in continuing dance –
this is God.

The Tornado

Funneling out of a starless sky
the wind raged
across a desperate prairie
rifling dust toward
a doomed solitary house
flinching in darkness.

*I remember holding the baby
at the door
then I woke up in the hospital,
I still can't remember
in between*
She says sixty years later.

Searching by lantern
they found others
buried in prairie mud.

Morning sun betrayed them.
Everything, but numbness,
was gone.

Even now the pasture lies bare.
Topsoil will not return
to that swath of destruction,
the trees twisted still
in some mutant gesture
to the tyranny
of that April night.

Cousins at Play

Riding yellow Tonka trucks
and John Deere green
tractors, they relish red
dirt bulldozing piles
on their knees, plowing
make-believe fields
like their sullied forefathers.

Calico kittens tangle
chasing tired grasshoppers
for fun – one boy stands
apart cranking the rusty
cistern pump handle,
his red wagon upset
on trampled sulphur grass.

An old dinner bell dangles
atop cedar poles
arching the dusty path
of home.

Forbidden

Beside moss-covered rocks,
pushing up through a bed
of decaying oak leaves
and acorns shrouded
in effluent humus,
a pair of cardinals flurry
through irregular limbs,
disrupting a creek
trickling
into obscurity,
we lay under silent
– and twisted cedars.

Little Boy Shucking Corn

A little boy shucking corn
by the burn pile out back of a broken house
stands knee-deep in silken husks.
Stalks fly in evening breeze
as he cleans yellow ears as long as his arm.
His spotted puppy sits atop his metronomic tail
fixated on the silent harvest.

A dad glances through the kitchen glass
to check on the progress of his boy.
August crickets sound and evening doves coo.
A meadowlark sits on a fence post.
Somewhere in approaching darkness,
a quail calls her covey.

Unaware of falling sky about them,
the boy concentrates on the tassels
to make ready the evening meal.
The dad knows his days are not long.
Their time will end and this place will be abandoned.
This evening will only be memory.

He knows strand by strand
his boy is becoming a man,
but tonight he is just thankful for the corn.

Wild Red Darkness

Nothing makes a sound in the night like the wind does.

— Bob McDill

Echoes

Tucked away
within the oaks,
daffodils outline
the residue
of a homestead.

A gravel road
winds to a stop
at the gate, a
rock fence marks
their isolation.

Like the house
a family is gone,
but new spring grass
returns alongside
a cracked foundation.

Dogwood buds
frame the yard
in colors where
children once voiced
a future.

Their absence echoes
in the wind,
speaks still,
defines them at play,
at work.

The barn resists –
brindled timbers dissolve
clinging
to each other
even as they falter.

Blue River

She calls me to secluded pools
along quiet shores
beneath canopies of White Oak
and Red Cedar.

My pace slows —
thoughts diminish,
sounds hush
in this cloistered place.

I sit in shadows smoking
a soft cigar,
the full moon peaking
above the ridge.

Beyond the dense timber,
purling water
and tree frogs abide
a humble campfire.

I have no need tonight
for noise,
no desire
for that other life.

Only primal sounds matter,
these ancient rituals
merging fire and water,
earth and sky.

What We Have Lost

What we have lost
lives only in memory,
in longing for wilder days
before greed
overran us, before time
became madness, before life
became a sales job,
before our vain scrambling
devoured us, before we
paraded our chicanery
for the world to bear witness
to our suicidal march.

What we have lost
is not recoverable
despite naive optimism
that proclaims a virtual reality
based on new technologies
that build illusionary economies
spurred by willful ignorance
of Nature's truth,
our hubris that promises new
frontiers and endless resources
just around the bend.

What we have lost
is a shirtless sun-tanned boy
standing knee-deep midstream
holding a cane pole, line
reaching into a swirling maroon eddy
as sundown descends
over graying green hills
secluded in transient air.

What we have lost
is the possibility that something
other than human frailty
moves us.

Summer Moon

The wind blew strong all day, blew
even stronger as afternoon faded
to evening, then, grudgingly fell
by degrees until finally calm covers
the water around me – only slight
whispering breaths now, the silence
before curtain rise when actors
appear on stage – the red moon rising
in the southeast, hovering the treeline,
red beams bleed across the water,
a blood trail to my heart, red moon
slowly lifting, slowly fading,
rising, as wind spurts across water,
as if in applause.

Summer Squall

Standing on a sandy rise,
endless prairie dark at her back,
bluestem bows like paupers
before a terrible Lord.

Unflinching, she scans
charcoal skies billowing,
scarred hands finger coarse denim.

Her back straightens,
a faded red flannel shirttail flapping,
chestnut hair swirling
at the mercy of wind.

The Fire Girl

In a former life she was a servant
charged with keeping fire.

See her master the task:
She enters the woods
gathers limbs for sacrifice
sorts them to piles
places them like a mason
setting stones in a wall
designed to outlive its maker.

She tends fire as if her life
depends on it —
circles the pit stirring coals
moving each bough
close to center flame —
the flame that will not go out
on her watch,
the flame that burns time,
consumes eternity,
that renders her life meaningful
so long as the fire
does not go out.

Shadows Across Junipers

Stretching west to east,
encroaching darkness
disfigures, discolors.

These shadows bring new
ways of seeing,
discourage my tendencies
to investigate *how it should be*
challenge my small ways
of knowing,
free me
to accept *how it is* —

to accept myself
even as I acknowledge shadows
now enveloping you.

Pastels

Twilight sky blends
to newness.

Every sundown
is unique,
varietal, endless.

Tonight the softness
clarifies
in surprising hues.

A mountain road
leads me home
past dark leafless timber,

past questions
that have no answer,

questions
that need not be asked.

Creek

Trickling stream
resisting summer drought,
nearly spent now,
drips
on moss and flintrock
as wind sings hope
of September rain
to bathe hay fields,
replenish depths
we only imagine –
buried
like the face of God.

Of Streams

When we refuse
    to hear streams
purling
    over rocks
the water
    murmuring
forward
    keening
downward,
    thrumming
in lonely
    subdued
measures,
    then we fail
to sense life,
    to know our
time-bound
    selves
trickling
    along
in hope
    over, around
and beyond
    the rocky
contours
    that shape
existence.

Thus the Dust

rains fine powder
grains
over plowed ground,
ground
plowed by hard-thinking pilgrims
who stopped here
at this place
to carve themselves
destiny
rehearsing
the dictates of Eden
relying on grit
willed to them
by their forebears,
that, and a native ability
to ignore pain
long enough to plow new rows,
long enough to start over
despite what dust
declares,
regardless death-shades
hovering.

Gone by Morning

Like stone, an old man
sits head-bowed, alone
beside dwindling flame
in memory pangs.

How many nights
has he sat with only
the obscure company
of a truck radio?

How many nights
has he camped
by this river-curve
hearing strange sounds

midst heart beats
and keening water,
his body aching
for morning?

Late Summer Nights

Humidity falls grudgingly
beneath a gibbous moon.

Sweaty horse flesh thickens
the air like cream. Tree frogs

and cicadas chatter like friends.
Phantom dark appears —

nimble ghosts dance from pecan
to oak to elm and back

erasing our false sense of space
and time. Harnessed

electricity hinders our knowing.
Spirits play hide and seek

with us in drooping sunflowers
and fescue gone to seed

where fat grasshoppers wait
death in morning dew.

Sleeping Out Under Stars

On a flatbed
wheat truck –
sideboards stored away
after harvest –
it is August now.

We lay bare
in night-heat
beneath uncountable stars
boring down
in radiant glory.

Hearing night-sounds
in the grass
we look above – transfixed
by the grandeur
of the unknown.

Nearly Angels

We are nearly angels –
I've been told.

We should dominate
the earth, then –
I have heard.

But other voices
whispering
in night-breezes say

we are part
of an unimaginable whole –

grains of sand,
drops in a river,
stars in countless galaxies –

say only fools
wish to trade places
with angels.

Forest Song

Yearn for silence beneath pines:
a forest floor meshed with fauna –
mossy rocks, oak, elm, locust, hackberry
intensify hushed tones.

Cling to fleeting moments
when calm erases commotion
you carry, clamor that wears you
until the fear of sitting still
and knowing yourself dissipates

until you find courage to change,
to restore your false self
in the silent truth proclaimed
beneath a canopy of pines.

November Night

In darkness, wait for your soul
on a November night. Frost murmuring, scratches
your feet while the moon
reminds you of your solitude,
your private journey into great
silent darkness to confirm
what can be found only
after waiting in cold moonlight
to learn what *cannot* be
known – after praying
under bright pagan stars.

Blackjacks Late in Winter

I admire old brown leaves
that will not fall,
those stubborn few that hang
until springtime buds
finally force them
off their branches.

They fall then to other uses.
They proudly resist
then die
as they have lived –
generously –
with the dignity of sacrifice.

Cimarron

A wildness that will not fade
calls in crimson twilight.

Our tangled roots of dirt and desire and denial
are embedded in cyclical rhythms
linked to the full moon shining
over Cherokee County, pulling
the Cimarron River along
to the Arkansas, filtering sand from clay,
leaving the heron a feast,
the mallard a respite.

Survivors know these rhythms –
these voices calling out in wild red darkness.

Singing of Transience

The wind is our friend, anyway, he thought.
Then he added, sometimes.

> – Hemingway's Santiago
> *The Old Man and the Sea*

Birth Song

The open road accommodates
my nascent mood between
new spring and old winter.

Early buds emerge like hope,
yet hesitate – brightly fixed
to stark branches.

Green grass arrives in disguise
beneath rude stalks.

Uprooted, I slowly drive
back-country roads –
Allman Brothers playing
at the edge of consciousness.

I pass through haze filtering
morning sun-riffs penetrate
trying to raise, to engender.

I taste flavors floating
to my window,
curling around my lips.

The Wounds of Oklahoma

This land makes you bleed:
drops coagulate
hard like adobe
in brazen sun.

The heart, too, follows
hard after dripping pain
into dull burdens
that stoop shoulders,
buckle knees,
humble you down
in simple honesty,
shape the will
toward submission –
grateful –
just to survive.

In Memoriam

We call a place beautiful because of its power.
We call a place home because of desire.
We assign meaning to something austere,
a violent, unforgiving legacy,
a red land that beckons
in haunted verses replayed in memoriam.

Imagine forces harsh enough to propel sleepy
Hungarians to leave all they knew,
to board ship, cross alien waters
to relocate in a world only imagined.

Consider the indifferent fortune that coincided
with the opening of the Cherokee Strip,
one people replacing another.

The new place has water; a creek divides
the section like an artery sustaining a desert.
The family stopped there and put in stakes
laying claim to a dusty crucible.

They enslaved themselves to soil.
They bargained with fortune by trading wheat
and alfalfa for native grass.

A family defined itself in those old hills
that bump along a venerable prairie.

It was home but now we look at the ruins
and see how the wilderness refused to surrender
to the plow, how Time only leased a space.

That was the Promised Land, our place
where destinies were forged,
a place where wind blows like the voice
of some terrifying god, a sadistic cosmos
that bends men and laughs at their repeated efforts
to stand straight, an eternal power
that marks men in tragic rhythms
and burgeoning red necks.

They washed the grime away
in the gypsum waters of Green Leaf Creek,
an oasis lined with cottonwoods
where Native families once lived on sandy beds.

Talk was rough, imagination hindered,
money scarce. The family dissolved.
Some died. Some went to war. Some went urban.
But none of them could forget that place.

One remained. Like his father and his grandfather
he held to the place as long as he could –
castrating steers, harvesting wheat, baling hay,
rebuilding machinery, tightening fences,
washing away parched dirt at the end of a windy day,
always accommodating the wind.

He bankrupted himself at least twice working
himself coarse. As stubborn as quartz
underlying a sandy ledge, he dug in and worked.

His wife went away. His children grew up.
He noticed he had fewer neighbors.
He borrowed more money and praised God
for a good wheat crop, then watched the market fall.
He sold a few remaining steers, went broken and sullied
to The City to find work, waiting to one day
go back to the only place he understands
to try again until he is buried in those sandy hills.

We left footprints in those borrowed lands.
We were marked by red dirt that will not be expunged.
Its residue reminds us what we have stubbornly
refused to hear, that we are transitory,
that earth is not ours – something the wind
has been speaking for centuries, something
we now realize, in memoriam.

Horses Grazing in a Country Cemetery

Oblivious to sacred markers
protruding out of the plots
their tails brush staid epitaphs aside.

Turning Maple leaves fall
on un-kept grassy knolls.
A failed fence with rusted,
broken hinges deteriorates.
Old weather takes its toll
on pine picket slats faded gray.

Like visitants from another realm,
they feed on the outgrowth
of dearly departed souls
who must now look down
in amusement since none
but the dying visit the dead.

Funeral Song

We the living huddle now
looking forlorn at a brown box
feeling wind at our backs,
come together beside puffy cedars
and a red-dirt mound.

For us this singing land
is sufficient, soft creek water
a blessing.

We find peace in prairie skies,
hope in evening stars.

For us the cold moon
and white sun are friends.

We dare not defy elements
that shape destiny,
but simply accept the logic
of earth and sky
as more than adequate,
reason enough to go on,
to love, to work,
to die old and content.

Requiem for the Wounded

She released two doves
when the preacher quit his words.

They all stood around his grave
hands in pockets
waiting to go.

One dove flew upward
away to some place
they imagined.

The second struggled
to get air-born
then crashed headlong
into a granite gravestone
just a few feet away.

Dying in dust,
it flapped useless wings
and they thought then
it was time to go.

Moonlight

Just a sliver
of light
tips toward us
sitting fireside
watching smoke
rise gently
past the tree-line
above hills
to the stars –
incense returning
to vials
from the temple
of the gods
of Autumn.

Red Dirge

Red-tipped fescue,
red sumac, ivy,
cedar bark and berries –
even the water is red
like old blood spilled
in Autumn rituals –
blood as familiar
as it is foreign, strange,
like turning leaves.

Tree Frogs

They screech
in violent unison,
singing death
trying to outpace
the wind.

Trilling
in desperation
they sound
a short summer
destiny.

Like dripping water,
that unending
lullaby
of the sandy bottom
warns.

The killing frost
falling
beneath a harvest moon
hovers
in the wind.

That Which Clings

Stick-tights cling to socks,
leggings and boot strings
as I explore emptiness,
this absent space –
this presence –
these jutting rocks
on the sauntering plain,
the dying briars
matted against red rock
and prickly pear,
bluestem dancing
in haunted rhythms
under a diminished sun,
lingering daylight.

I walk this vapid prairie
sensing vacancies within,
discerning essence,
the self whole, defined
in September wind
scolding, consoling:
there are things learned
only by failure
and things failed
despite the learning.

Of Desire: or What Foxes Do

Foxes Digging Mice
– Bronze by Kenneth R. Bunn
Gilcrease Museum, Tulsa Oklahoma

Every time I see art, see beauty,
I think of you. How can I forget you
when the guts of raw survival
won't let me – and this
seems reason enough not to.

I've wandered through this museum
imagining you each step,
remembering how we used to be.
You are too real, so I half-look
at the paintings, afraid to stop
and know them, your ghost haunts.

Finally I come to a window
in a back corner, and I pause, look
out over the Gilcrease Hills.
Leaves are flying off the trees.
It is December and new weather
is arriving, but it feels like the same
clichéd emotion, trite for everyone
except the sophomore writer
who does not understand
his novelty is not that special.
But how can you tell one locked
in the grip of passion that pain
and truth are like lead to the pencil?

How does one move beyond
the aesthetics of space and time,
how to be raw and survive?

Beneath wind-blown trees I notice
Fox Digging Mice, and I see
a lover lost in desire, digging
for any morsel of hope – digging
because digging is beyond thought,
digging because digging mice
is what foxes do.

River Song

Motion helps us
understand –
helps us cope.

It is right to move
downstream
to avoid stasis

to resist delusions
of permanence,
the futility

of holding on.
To feel the flowing
around me,

through me
is life.
To be one

with the current –
this much
is real.

Grace Strokes

There are bright cloudless mornings
that overshadow your mood,
create within your confusion a respite
where breath and hope coexist
the way a silent canoe glides
through water at sunrise, my rowing
my attempts at faith, striking the oar
into the water, breaking the glass surface
that holds so much promise but keeps it
a lifetime away, the transparent wall
between me and happiness.

I push the oar deeper below the surface,
past broken-ness and feel energy
swirl, transfer upward to forearms
through synapses into shoulder,
into heart, into brain – and the act triggers
memories with each stroke and I cringe
at how it is I have come to this place
and time of losing – but I also know
each stroke propels me further from pain
and closer to tomorrow where clouds
merge with sunshine into bliss,
where memories, like oars dipping
in mysterious water, grace me past
the pain, past fearful claims of a future.

What Wind Takes

On these first days of winter,
on these grief-filled days
when confusion swirls
like December bluster
through leafless trees
and bent grass –

    realize

wind takes you to new
places for new purpose.
Remember spring returns
and the life you crave
is possible now in death
flying all around you.

Winter Stories

What dreams now fly
away in southern wind
skirting across a pond
where below dark water
even darker truth seems.

A country dream home,
an inviting front porch,
a wind chime mitigating
this dark afternoon.

I left the others inside
with Christmas carols –
too cheery for today.

Standing in the yard
I admire a mature, solid
pine. I feel wind correct
false hopes, the chimes
now in pace with my
shifting heart gearing down
for a month of blue –
somehow appropriate
for winter stories, told
and told again, with hopes
of something new in
the familiar – like pine cones
or somber notes chiming.

Compensation

I come here because I want to hear rain
dripping through pines when no one else
is around, to feel December wind

wrap around me while I gather twigs,
damp and soggy needles to kindle fire
to thaw my bones, withdrawn
like pine cones in lonely chill.

Smoke brims my eyes, tickles my lungs.
Chartreuse flames lick oblate cones
as compensation for solitude.

New silence hovers in the pines –
steady, unhurried rain patting
the roof, an occasional flame
pops in remaining coals.

Wind Song

Tell me secrets
in the night sky;
whisper lines
the ancients knew.

Night voices sing
hope, fire
imagination,
kindle souls

into red-flame
that destroys
but purges,
re-seeds,

creates –
these Saturnian
voices singing
of transience.

ACKNOWLEDGMENTS

Many thanks to the editors of the following journals where the following poems first appeared:

Crosstimbers: "The Old Home Place" and "The Tornado"

Desert Candle: "Wind Song"

Flint Hills Review: "Cimarron"

Meridian Anthology of Contemporary Poetry: "Of Streams" and "Blue River"

Muse Squared: "What We Have Lost" and "November" and "Of Streams"

Oklahoma Today: "Compensation" and "Indian Paintbrush"

Poesia: "Pastels" and "That Which Clings"

Red Dirt Anthology, 2005: "Red Dirge"

Red River Review: "Building Barbed Wire" and "Little Boy Shucking Corn" and "The Witness Tree" and "Dressing Catfish" and "Funeral Song"

Two Southwests: "Grace Strokes" and "That Which Clings"

Westview: "What We Have Lost" and "Forbidden"

Second edition Interior art by Duane Hada
www.rivertowngallery.com

Special thanks to Dorothy Alexander and Devey Napier of Village Books Press, whose first edition of *Way of the Wind* welcomed me to the publishing game. Their kindness to emerging poets is gracious and boundless.

About The Author

Ken Hada is the author of seven collections of poetry. His work has been recognized and awarded by the National Western Heritage Museum and Cowboy Hall of Fame, Western Writers of America the Oklahoma Center for the Book, SCMLA Prize for Poetry and on *The Writer's Almanac*. From his home in Pottawatomie County, Oklahoma, he offers a weekly podcast – *The Sunday Poems*. Additional information is available at kenhada.org.

www.ingramcontent.com/pod-product-compliance
Lightning Source LLC
Chambersburg PA
CBHW052110070526
44584CB00017B/2426